All About

Dwayne Johnson

Dwayne Johnson Biography Children's Book for Kids (With Bonus! Coloring Pages and Videos)

By All About Books

Before You Go Any Further, Get Your <u>FREE Gift</u>!
(Worth $67)

Never Fear "The Call" from the School or the Hospital Again!
How to Effectively Communicate With Your Child About
Safety in a <u>Fun Way!</u>

Did you know if children are not taught properly about safety at a young age, it can potentially lead to reckless, dangerous behaviors even when they become a teenager or an adult?

Never fear "the call" from the school or the hospital with this comprehensive video course!

It'll teach you how to communicate effectively with your young ones about safety without boring them!

(Limited-Time FREE Gift)

Get It Before It Expires Here:

<u>https://allaboutbookseries.com/freegift/</u>

Table of Contents

Disclaimer and Note to Readers:

This book is an unofficial tribute book to Dwayne Johnson from a fan to support his legacy.

The information in this book is provided for educational and entertainment purposes only.

The information in this book has been compiled from reliable sources. It is accurate to the best of the author's knowledge; however, the author cannot guarantee its accuracy and validity and cannot be held liable for any errors or omissions.

If you use the information contained in this book, you agree that the author is free from and not liable for any damages, costs, and expenses, including any legal fees, potentially resulting from applying any of the information provided by this guide.

The disclaimer applies to any damages or injury caused by the use and application, whether directly or indirectly, of any advice or information presented, whether for breach of contract, tort, neglect, personal injury, criminal intent, or under any other cause of action. You agree to accept all risks of using the information presented inside this book.

If an individual cites this publication as the source of information, it does not imply that the author or publisher endorse the individual or organization's knowledge. This book is an unofficial fan tribute and has not been approved or endorsed by Dwayne Johnson or his associates.

The Rock at Ringside by Photographer: Tom Kralidis licensed under the <u>Creative Commons</u> <u>Attribution-Share Alike 3.0 Unported</u> license.

Introduction to Dwayne Johnson

Dwayne "The Rock" Johnson is an American actor and businessman. He used to be a professional wrestler, and to date, he is still regarded as one of the greatest wrestlers ever. He spent eight years as a professional WWE wrestler before transitioning to the acting industry.

His films have brought in a revenue of over $10.5 billion. As a result, he is one of the highest-paid actors in the world.

Growing up, he wanted to be a football player. He was on the right track for this, as he even played college football and won a National Championship. Unfortunately, he didn't become a football player due to some injuries.

He started wrestling in 1996, became famous, and then left in 2004. He returned in 2011 and kept making appearances till 2019, when he retired.

As an actor, he is famous for his roles in the *Fast and Furious* franchise and *Jumanji*.

Who is Dwane "The Rock" Johnson

http://allaboutbookseries.com/WhoisTheRock

Dwayne Johnson's Early Childhood

Dwayne Douglas Johnson was born on May 2, 1972, in Hayward, California. His father, Rocky Johnson (born Wayde Douglas Bowles), is a Canadian from Scotia, Nova. His mother, Ata Johnson, is Samoan.

His father was a professional wrestler who won a lot of trophies. He, along with his partner Tony Atlas, was the first black champion in WWE history.

Rocky Johnson met Ata while partnered with wrestling "high chief" Peter Maivia in a tag team. Peter Maivia invited him to spend the night with his family since he was in town for a night. It was then he met Ata, and the couple fell in love. Ata didn't like Rocky Johnson when they first met, but like a classic troupe, they fell in love with each other.

At that time, Rocky was married to Una, his first wife, a Canadian. Peter Maivia was firmly against the relationship, primarily because Rocky was a wrestler. Rocky later divorced his first wife and married Ata Maivia in December 1978.

Ata's parents were against the union at first. People thought it was because Rocky Johnson was a wrestler, always on the road, and they didn't want that kind of life for their daughter.

Dwayne's grandfather, Peter Maivia, was a wrestling star. He achieved fame from wrestling. He was also a wrestling promoter. When he died, he left the business to his wife, Leah. She was a hands-on business owner. She was the first woman wrestling promoter, and she was incredibly brilliant at it. She became the Vice President of the National Wrestling Alliance, and she even brought a weekly wrestling TV show to Hawaii. She organized the "High Chief Peter Maivia Memorial Tribute Show." It was a yearly event that featured wrestling geniuses from all over the world, including Andre the Giant and Ric Flair.

While Dwayne Johnson was growing up, he lived in Auckland with his mother's family. He attended school there and even played rugby.

The Johnson family moved a lot, so he changed schools a lot. While the family lived in North Carolina, he studied at Montclaire Elementary School in Charlotte, North Carolina, before moving to Hamden, Connecticut. There, He studied at Shepherd Glen Elementary School and Hamden Middle School. He also went to President William McKinley High School in Honolulu, Hawaii, and later Glencliff High School and McGavock High School in Nashville, Tennessee, and Freedom High School in Bethlehem, Pennsylvania.

Dwayne Johnson grew up watching his father "work the gimmick." This means that they had to keep up with appearances. Rocky Johnson was famous in wrestling; a lot of people assumed he was rich. So, Rocky kept up with the facade and taught Dwayne to do the same.

Even though they lived in a shabby apartment, they had a fancy car, which led people to think they were really rich.

Question to Ponder: Have you ever done anything to make people think you were richer than you were?

This led Dwayne to make a lot of bad decisions. He was arrested multiple times. Most of his crimes included theft, shoplifting, check fraud, and fighting.

Dwayne Johnson was an early bloomer. He often attracted the attention of older women and got a rise out of older boys. The fact that he looked older than he was greatly attributed to this. Dwayne had a temper, and he didn't mind getting into fights.

One time, he confronted a guy for spreading rumors that he was using steroids for bulking up. They got into a fight, and he beat up the guy, who was equally large. Things went south, however, when the guy slumped and cracked his head against the locker. Dwayne got suspended for this.

Question to Ponder: Have you ever been in a fight? What caused it?

In his sophomore year, Dwayne joined the amateur wrestling team. On his first day on the team, he defeated the school's heavyweight champion. For him, it was so easy; he didn't want to do wrestling again, so he quit the team.

Football Career

In his junior year of high school, Dwayne joined the football team. He was a promising football player. He played as a defensive linebacker, and he was good at it. He was the team captain. He finished high school football, so, it was no surprise that in his final year of high school, he received a lot of offers from Division I collegiate programs. He was all American; he was the eighth-best player in all of Pennsylvania.

He received a scholarship offer to play at the University of Miami, which he took. He majored in criminology and physiology.

He was the only freshman who was going to play with the team. He was not redshirted. However, things went south.

On the last day of his first preseason with the University of Miami Hurricanes, Johnson suffered an injury during practice. It was a full blown-out shoulder separation that required surgery. Johnson was meant to be the only freshman who started that year, but due to his shoulder, he could not play that season. This was the beginning of many injuries in his time at Miami. It affected him a lot in school. He began to miss practice and then classes; he sat in his dorm room feeling sorry for himself while pretending that everything was fine. He didn't know how to cope because he had tied his identity to being a football player on the field. Now, he was a football player who was not playing. He was just as ordinary as the next kid.

He didn't see the need to pay attention to his academics. He even missed his final exam that year. Coach Oregon mentioned that it could have been an All-American season for Johnson that year.

Question to Ponder: How would you feel if you could not be part of something you were excited about?

The following year, Johnson came back stronger. He put his all into school and practice; he got better. However, he got a new teammate, Warren Sapp, who took over Johnson's job. He also sustained a lot of other injuries on his knee and had to have reconstructive surgeries five times. He also suffered a torn Achilles heel.

Dwayne Johnson played a backup role and only started one game in his four years at the University of Miami.

In his final year, he suffered from two ruptured discs and had to go to rehabilitation after each game.

Due to his injuries and lack of playing time, Dwayne Johnson didn't make it into the NFL to play professionally.

http://allaboutbookseries.com/DwayneFootball

Question to Ponder: Have you ever lost an opportunity because of something beyond your control? How would you feel if you were Dwayne and didn't get to the NFL even though you wanted to be a football player?

Aside from football, Dwayne Johnson was also a prolific speaker. He was one of the university's best speakers and often spoke to youths, advising them to stay in school and abstain from drugs.

After his college, Dwayne didn't get drafted to the NFL. However, he joined the Calgary Stampeders of the Canadian Football League as a linebacker.

When he got to Canada, the differences in their football games were glaring. In usual Dwayne fashion, he was adapting, or at least he thought he was, as he was assigned to the practice roster.

As a practice football player, Dwayne did not earn much. His take-home pay totaled $175 weekly in US dollars. It was not a lot, so he used to sell his free tickets to home games. As a practice player, he had a lot of free time, too, so he started to toy with the idea of wrestling in his. Unfortunately, there was no wrestling academy close to Calgary where he could practice.

Fortunately and unfortunately, due to a rule that restricted the number of non-Canadians that played in each Canadian team, he was removed two months into the season.

On the flight home from Calgary, Dwayne started to think of what to do with his life. At this point, it was obvious he would not be a football player. So, he decided he was going to be a wrestler. It sounded ridiculous, but his girlfriend at that time, Dany, was supportive, and she told him to go ahead.

He informed his parents about his career change and didn't give them the opportunity to question it.

His mom was supportive of the career change, but his dad was not so enthusiastic about his going into wrestling.

Early Wrestling Career

As Dwayne started to transition into wrestling, he got a job at a fitness center. He was an instructor.

During that period, he started to train for wrestling. His first training was with Ron Slinker, a former wrestler and a friend of his dad's. His first session went well; it gave him clarity. "At that very moment, I knew; this was what I was born to do."

He kept practicing, and as time went on, he was adding his own touch to things. It was brilliant.

When it came to picking a ring name, his mom suggested "Rocky Maivia." Dwayne didn't want that. He was trying to break into wrestling without using his family name. He didn't want to cash on the reputation of his father or grandfather; he wanted to make a name all by himself.

When he started to get better, Dwayne decided that he was going to call veteran wrestler Pat Patterson. Pat had wrestled with his grandfather and was a friend of the family. He wanted to do it on his own, so he invited Pat to watch him practice.

On that day, he wrestled against his father, soul man Rocky Johnson. At the end of the practice, he asked Pat if he was going to make it in the business; Pat told him he would be okay and to keep practicing.

With the help of Pat Paterson, Dwayne participated in several tryout matches with the World Wrestling Foundation in 1996. During this time, he used his real name, "Dwayne Johnson," to contest. In his first match, he fought in front of fifteen thousand people. They were unenthusiastic to see him. After he was introduced as "Dwayne Johnson, from Miami, FL, 270 pounds," they said things like, "Go back to Miami, loser!" Dwayne did not pay attention to the trash talk.

Question to Ponder: Have you ever been in a situation where people were discouraging you before you even had the chance to prove yourself? How did you feel?

Dwayne walked into the ring, and for eight minutes, he wrestled with his opponent. Then he defeated his opponent, and the crowd applauded.

Question to Ponder: How do you think Dwayne felt proving to the crowd that he was not a loser?

After he was announced as the winner and he left the ring, a lot of people came to congratulate him.

He beat "The Brooklyn Brawler" at an in-house show on March 10, 1996.

His next opponent was Chris Candido, an athletic guy; he defeated Dwayne with a Frankensteiner off the top rope.

After his tryouts, he got his report card. He had a great tryout, but the promoters didn't think he was ready for the big leagues of the World Wrestling Federation. So, they sent him to Memphis, the United States World Wrestling Alliance.

This is The Rock

http://allaboutbookseries.com/ThisisTheRock

United States World Wrestling Alliance

It would have been a big deal for Dwayne to join the big leagues, but Memphis was what he needed, so he went there. Dwayne left for Memphis on May 13, 1966, in his Isuzu Rodeo truck which he used his savings to buy. He felt like the happiest person in the world.

He got to Memphis and decided that he was going to change his ring name. While Dwayne Johnson was a beautiful name, it didn't look like it would cut the ring, so he changed his name to "Flex Kavana."

Flex Kavana made his debut in the wrestling industry the day after Dwayne arrived in Memphis. He was part of a tag team, partnered with "Too Sexy" Brian Christopher. The first match was against Jerry "the King" Lawler and Bill Dundee. It was wild and fun.

During his stay at Memphis, Dwayne worked hard. He earned $40 each night that he worked and tried to make extra by selling pictures of himself. He also kept calling JJ Dillion of WWF and kept informing him that he had improved in wrestling and he was available if there was any space in WWF. Dwayne was also setting goals for himself.

Question to Poder: Do you think it was a good thing that Dwayne Johnson kept positioning himself for better opportunities?

Six months after he arrived in Memphis, JJ Dillon called him. He was to fly to Columbus, Ohio, for a fight against Owen Hart. When he got to the arena, he saw that Owen's left hand was in a cast. Normally, in wrestling, the left hand is the hand the opponent grabs. However, Dwayne felt that he didn't want to hurt Owen more than he was already hurt, so he grabbed the right hand. To professional wrestlers, it looked like Dwayne didn't know what he was doing, so Owen told him that it was the wrong hand. Dwayne told him he knew, but the other hand was hurt, so Owen started laughing. Dwayne felt embarrassed. "Here I was trying to be the nice guy, and I got duped."

Question to Ponder: How would you have felt in Dwayne's situation?

The match ended, and Dwayne got encouraging words from Owen Hart. He told him he was better than most of the guys on the World Wrestling Federation roster. Owen had shared the compliment with Vince Mahone. Dwayne was on cloud nine. Nothing could rain on his parade at that point.

Then, Pat Patterson called him. Pat told him that he had to work on his punches. When he got to Memphis, he started practicing his punches. He made a promise that he was going to throw the best punches.

Two weeks after his fight with Owen Hart, JJ Dillon called again. They wanted him out of Memphis. According to them, Memphis was not conducive to his development as they assumed. They were taking him to World Wrestling Federation's corporate headquarters in Connecticut. It offered training with state-of-the-art equipment. WWF promised to sort out the technicalities of Dwayne Johnson leaving Memphis; Dwayne packed and left; he saw no reason to stay.

World Wrestling Federation: Rocky Maivia

Dwayne moved to Stanford, Connecticut, and continued training. Two months after his move, he was placed on the roster. The plan when he started training was that he would debut in November's Survivor series. His persona as "Flex Kavana" was gone, too. He had to pick a new name. The office suggested "Rocky Maivia" just as his mother had earlier suggested, but he refused. The office took it on themselves to convince him about the name.

"Together, they tried to convince me that there was nothing shameful or insulting about using the name 'Rocky Maivia.' 'We're not asking you to go into the ring barefoot like your grandfather did or do a Samoan dance or anything like that. And we're not asking you to do the jabs or Ali shuffle as your father did. You're a man on your own now. This is just a way of showing your respect.'"

Dwayne felt convinced to use the name, especially because his father loved the name, and it was something his grandfather would have liked if he were still alive. So, Rocky Maivia it was.

On November 16, 1966, in New York at Madison Square Garden, Rocky Maivia made his debut in the Survivor series of the World Wrestling Foundation. It was huge.

Question to Ponder: How would you have felt if you were Dwayne Johnson debuting on a larger scale? Do you think Dwayne was excited about this?

Dwayne also found out that based on the script for the survivor series, he was going to win. He mentioned that it was not the winning that excited him. This is because he had to follow a script and know his role. He was not better than anyone else. He was excited at the thought of what it would mean to be "Rocky Maivia— champion of the Survivor series."

When he won the Survivor series, it was obvious to anyone watching at that moment that Rocky Maivia, the rookie who won the Survivor series on his debut, was going to be around for a while.

After the Survivor series, Dwayne's workload increased. He went on his first international tour. It was nice. However, fans didn't know a lot about him. He always kept to himself.

After a while, Bret Hart, another wrestler, decided to make things easy for Dwayne. He would sit beside him during bus rides, talk to him, and introduce him to others. Owen Hart was also the same, except Owen had a mean streak, and he expressed it through practical jokes. And yes, the cast on his arm was not the last one.

During Dwayne's first international tour, at the main event in Dubai, he had another experience. It was an eight-man tag team that consisted of wrestling's biggest stars, including Undertaker, Owen Hart, and Bret Hart. Then there was a newbie, Rocky Maivia. As the match progressed, Undertaker and Bret Hart were doing some serious damage to Owen's leg. Then it was Dwayne's turn. He got into the ring and dragged Owen's leg, the same one Undertaker and Bret Hart had worked on. However, Owen was clowning around. The leg had obviously been hurting before Dwayne started working on it, trying to abuse it. So, Dwayne was confused. After a while, Owen said to Dwayne, "Shoot me off; I'll reverse you; give me a bug tackle." So, Dwayne went with this. Normally in wrestling, when a wrestler gives a big tackle, he goes down with authority. However, when Dwayne gave Owen the big tackle, instead of Owen going down hard, he went down in a slow-motion fall. It was hilarious; the audience and the guys in the ring started to laugh. Dwayne laughed, too.

Dwayne Johnson had an exciting career. There were highs on the job; it also came with lows. One of the low points was when Shawn Michaels relinquished the federation championship. He was not defending the title. So, it fell on Dwayne. Around the same time, Triple H was going to drop the intercontinental championship to Dwayne. Wrestling fans started to feel like the World Wrestling Foundation forced Rocky Maivia down their throats.

At the same time, the wrestling industry was going through changes. There was "Stone Cold" Steve Austin, who was playing the anti-hero, so many wrestling fans loved him. Rocky Maivia was a baby face to the "T." He was the good boy that would help older women cross the road. Frankly, fans were tired of that. They used to be excited to see Steve Austin cussing. They would say things like, "Rocky Maivia? Forget it." Dwayne didn't mind. He turned up every time he had to work.

On March 27, 1997, in Chicago, the site for Wrestlemania XIII. Dwayne had invited his parents and then-girlfriend Dany. It was supposed to be a wonderful night as he was defending his intercontinental title from Iron Sheik. As he made his entrance, fans started to chant, "Rocky sucks, Rocky sucks."

Question to Ponder: What would you have done if you were in Dwayne's position at that point?

For Dwayne, the whole thing was confusing. His character was a babyface, the good guy. So why were fans against him? He thought he could win the match and make things smooth. So, he won the game and defended his title. When he was done, the crowd kept chanting, "Rocky Sucks." "Die, Rocky." At first, he tried to stay in character and smile. However, when so much violence is directed at someone, it's easy for that person to fall out of character. He stopped smiling. That spring, he dropped the Intercontinental title to Owen Hart and went home with a torn ligament in his knee. He was given eight weeks off for rehabilitation, so he stayed out of the spotlight. In those eight weeks, Rocky Maivia started to fade.

The Rock

During his break from the spotlight, Dwayne Johnson married his longtime girlfriend, Dany. The event was a sweet blend of Samoan and Cuban ceremonies. It was beautiful.

After the wedding, Dwayne was approached to switch from a babyface to a heel. Heels are generally the bad guys. He agreed, so he joined the Nation of Nomination, or the Nation for short. It was a militant faction of wrestling. They were organized and included different ethnicities.

For his first appearance as a heel, he did a "run in." Farooq, the guy who ran the Nation, was wrestling a guy named Chainz. Rocky ran into the ring and sent Chainz to rock bottom. It was confusing for fans because Rocky Maivia was a good guy. He was supposed to be helping Chainz. He beat Chainz and placed Farooq on Chainz, then left. Farooq won the match, but people were surprised that Dwayne made a move like that.

http://allaboutbookseries.com/NationofDomination

Dwayne Johnson was officially a heel, but he was concerned about the nation's image. He wanted to be the worst heel possible, but he didn't want to appear racist.

Question to Ponder: Have you ever been in a situation where the reputations of the people you hung out with affected how you were seen? What did you do?

So, Dwayne approached the head writer, then informed him that he wanted an interview to tell people why he joined the Nation. It was granted.

When he went for the interview, fans were yelling, "Rocky Sucks, die, Rocky" again. But this time, it didn't bother Dwayne. So, Farooq handed him the mic, and he began talking. The whole arena was quiet.

"Let me tell you, people, one thing... Go to hell!" He had the attention of the crowd then.

"That's the response I get from you people? After giving my blood, my sweat, and my tears? For months and months? Signs that say 'Die Rocky' and hearing 'Rocky sucks' across every arena in the country?"

The crowd started to chant, "Rocky sucks" again. Dwayne let them have their fun; then he delivered the message.

"I just want to make it perfectly clear, 'I may be a lot of things, but sucks isn't one of them.' Joining the Nation was not a white or black thing; it was a respect thing. One way or the other, from now on, Rocky Maivia is going to get respect...by any means possible."

In the months that came, he became the hottest heel in the industry.

The key moment for this change was when he cut into Steve Austin's promo. Steve, who was the intercontinental winner, was just coming back from injury. He was shooting a promo when Rocky walked in as if he owned the place. Then he said,

"I hate to rain on your little victory parade, but I just want to come out here and make a special note. Everybody knows that when I was World Wrestling Federation Champion, I was the best damn Intercontinental champion there ever was."

"Boooooo!" Steve responded.

"Stone Cold Steve Austin, I'm challenging you for the intercontinental championship, and if you have any manhood at all, you will accept my challenge."

"Booooooo!" Steve responded again.

So, Dwayne continued; then he used Steve's catchphrase against him. "That's the bottom line; Steve said so."

"And if you do accept my challenge, then your bottom line will be 'Stone Cold Has-been,' compliments of The Rock."

That was it for Dwayne Johnson. With that finishing line, Rocky Maivia became known as "The Rock." The Rock was Dwayne Johnson with his personality turned up.

Steve Austin accepted the challenge; this was what began the rivalry between The Rock and "Stone Cold" Steve Austin. The rivals gave wrestling fans content to look forward to.

http://allaboutbookseries.com/TheRockVSSteveAustin

One of the highlights of this rivalry is the popular pager incident that occurred on "Raw is War." The Rock was shooting a promo, and Steve Austin decided to cut the promo in half by ensuring that his big ugly mug was staring from the Titantron. This offended the Rock, so they began to square off. Things got heated when Stone Cold said, "When you're walking through the airport, Rock your pager goes off, and you look down to see 3:16."

3:16 is one of Steve Austin's catchphrases which means, "I just whooped your ass."

Steve Austin left the building, and not long after, The Rock's pager went off. Then he pushed the button and saw a paper that said 3:16. The Rock was mad that Stone Cold was trying to embarrass him on national TV So, The Rock turned around and saw Stone Cold trying to jump him. It was too late to protect himself. So, he got beaten on his promo, too.

Stone Cold Steve Austin accepts the match with The Rock. Stone Cold Steve Austin defeated The Rock in that match. He was still champion. Then there was a rematch, but Stone Cold forfeited the belt to the Rock.

The Rock had to defend his title as intercontinental champion against Ken Shamrock in 1998 at Royal Rumble. Steve Austin later defeated The Rock by elimination. On March 29 at Wrestlemania XIV, The Rock defeated Shamrock by disqualification once again to retain the title.

He later debuted a new Intercontinental Championship design. He later overthrew Faarooq as leader of the Nation of Domination to spark a feud between the two. Stone Cold Steve Austin accepted the match with The Rock. Stone Cold Steve Austin defeated The Rock in that match. He was still champion. Then there was a rematch, but Stone Cold forfeited the belt to the Rock.

The Rock had to defend his title as intercontinental champion against Ken Shamrock in 1998 at Royal Rumble. Steve Austin later defeated The Rock by elimination. On March 29 at Wrestlemania XIV, The Rock defeated Shamrock by disqualification once again to retain the title.

He later debuted a new Intercontinental Championship design.

By May 1998, The Rock had earned his fame, and everyone respected him. However, he had some animosity with members of The Nation, especially Farooq, the leader. He presented the other members with a Rolex and then gave Farooq a blown-up picture of him holding a championship belt. Farooq was not having it. Dwayne told him, "Farooq, you have three seconds, and the Rock means three seconds before the Rock lays the smackdown on your candy ass." The Rock began to count, but Farooq was not moved. The Rock smacked him, almost knocking him out. The other members of The Nation prevented the Rock from completing what he started with Farooq. That led to an official match where they could both fight.

He overthrew Farooq in the match, and he took over as leader of the Nation of Domination to spark a feud between the two.

Nation of Domination turns their back on Farooq

http://allaboutbookseries.com/NationTurnsBackonFaarooq

King of the Ring

After Defeating Farooq, The Rock continued to succeed in his endeavors. On June 28, 1998, The Rock joined King of the Ring. He had just recovered from the surgery to fix his torn knee ligament. He was ready to go into the ring and sacrifice everything to prove that he was the people's champion. He defeated Jabroni this and Jabroni that and went further to defeat Dan the Beast Severn. Then it was time for the final fight. His opponent was Ken Shamrock. Did I mention that they were rivals? Oh well, they are rivals.

The match with Ken Shamrock was going well. In fact, it was in The Rock's favor. Unfortunately, the Rock made an error, and Ken Shamrock put an ankle lock submission on The Rock. The Rock tapped out, and Ken Shamrock was the new king of the Ring.

The Rock vs. Ken Shamrock

http://allaboutbookseries.com/TheRockVSKenShamrock

Question to Ponder: Have you ever made a mistake that cost you a victory? How did it feel?

Shortly after Summerslam, The Rock formed a tag team with his former opponent, "Mankind." The duo was known as the "Rock and Sock" connection. They won the WWF World Championship for the first time after defeating Undertaker and Big Show on August 30, 1999. They performed different skits together, such as "This is your life," a critically acclaimed comedy skit that featured parodic versions of people from The Rock's past, like his high school girlfriend and coach, only for The Rock to insult them. It was hilarious.

Rock and Sock: This is your life

http://allaboutbookseries.com/RockandSock

The duo later lost their title to the New Age Outlaws. They won it again in October of 1999 before losing it to the Holly Cousins four days later.

The Rock's Career in the 2000s

The Rock entered the Royal Rumble match of January 2000. He, along with Big Show, was the final player. Big Show attempted a false finish, but it was countered by The Rock, who sent Big Show to the floor, and he emerged the winner.

Subsequently, Big Show provided footage that revealed that The Rock's feet hit the floor during the reversal attempt. Thus, Big Show claimed to be the owner of the title. The Rock and Big Show fought again at No way out, which Big Show won due to the influence of Shane McMahon. The Rock defeated Big Show again at Raw is War; then he got the right to face Triple H, who was WWF Champion.

The Rock: World Champion

In the succeeding weeks, the Rock and Triple H continued their feud. He finally won his fourth championship at Backlash on April 30 after Stone Cold Austin joined him. The following night, he successfully defended his title against Shane McMahon. At Summerslam, he defended his title against Kurt Angle and Triple H. At Unforgiven, he successfully defended the title against Kane, Benoit, and Undertaker.

He lost his title to Kurt Angle at No Mercy. He wrestled at a six-man "hell in a cell" match to win the WWF championship title at Armageddon. For most of 2001, The Rock and Kurt Angle rivaled for the WWF champion title. The pinnacle of this rivalry was at No Way Out, where he pinned Kurt to win his title for the sixth time.

He continued his feud with Stone Cold Steve Austin, to whom he lost his title. He was disqualified. During this time, he starred in *The Scorpion King*.

The Rock returned in July 2001. At that time, WWF was in a rivalry with World Championship Wrestling (WCW) and Extreme Championship Wrestling (ECW). However, WCW was bought by Vince McMahon and the WWF, and ECW went out of business in early 2001. Wrestlers who used to work with WCW and ECW were brought onto WWF television and formed The Alliance to compete with WWF in the storyline.

Dwayne Johnson later took a break to focus on his acting career. He returned in 2003 and fought against Hulk Hogan on an episode of Smackdown. He started a new persona known as Hollywood Rock. He also started a segment known as "Rock Concert," where he mocked fellow WWE performers and fans.

A Raw episode was dedicated to him for defeating Stone Cold Austin. It was titled "Rock Appreciation Night." A debuting Goldberg defeated the Rock. The Rock left to film "Walking Tall."

He made occasional appearances between 2003 and 2004. Later in 2004, the Rock's contract ended, and he started acting full time.

Between 2007 and 2009, he made a series of non-wrestling appearances. On March 29, 2008, The Rock appeared to induct his father, Rocky Johnson, and grandfather, High Chief Peter Maivia, to the Wrestling Hall of Fame.

On February 14, 2011, The Rock was announced as the host of Wrestlemania XXVII. He started a feud with John Cena. The rivals promised to meet at Wrestlemania the following year. The Rock and Cena fought together and often fought against each other, leading to Wrestlemania the following year.

The Rock defeated CM Punk to win his right WWE Championship. He resumed his rivalry with John Cena. Cena later defeated him at Wrestlemania 29. He was entitled to a rematch, but he didn't appear due to an injury that caused his tendons to tear during the match with Cena. He had to undergo surgery to fix it.

From 2014 to 2019, the Rock made a series of appearances at wrestling matches. In 2020, he made an appearance at Impact Wrestling.

Dwayne Johnson's Acting Career

As he was already well known due to his wrestling career, Dwayne was able to enter the Hollywood movie industry easily. He got a lot of acting offers from different studios, so he began his acting career while still into wrestling. He played his first role in 1999 when he acted as his own father (Rocky Johnson) in an episode of "That 70's Show." Close to a year later, Dwayne made an appearance in an episode of "Star Trek: Voyager" called Tsunkatse. In that episode, he played the role of an alien fighter who fought with the well-known character, seven of nine. He also got an offer in 2000 to host "Saturday Night Live," a comedy variety show. Dwayne had stated that when he originally got the offer, he fell out of his chair in utter disbelief.

Dwayne in the 2000s

Dwayne's acting career advanced greatly in the 2000s. He appeared in many movies and played various roles, which unlocked more job opportunities for him. Due to his wrestling career and large body build, Dwayne mostly starred in action movies that at times came with a mix of comedy. In 2001, he played the role of Mathayus, the scorpion king, in *The Mummy Returns* and, in the spinoff, *The Scorpion King* in 2002. The latter movie was where Dwayne had his first lead role as a villainous ruler and was able to show his great acting skills in this action fantasy genre. Although the ratings of the movie *The Scorpion King* weren't exactly high, he was paid 5.5 million US Dollars, which was the usual pay for most lead actors at that time. In 2003, he took on another lead role and played Berk, a bounty hunter, in the movie *The Rundown*. His love for action roles doesn't stop as we see Dwayne play the role of a former U.S. Soldier in the crime/action movie *Walking Tall*. Dwayne went on to star in so many other movies like *Be Cool*, where he played a supporting role, and in *Doom*, where he was to act as an antagonist in the movie. To show his diverse acting abilities, he played the role of a family man in *The Game Plan* and acted in comedy movies like *The Other Guys* (2010), *Tooth Fairy*, *Southland Tales* (2006), and many others.

Question to Ponder: How would you feel doing something new for the first time?

Dwayne's Career Breakthrough

Having acted for so many years, none of his movies had gained a lot of popularity, which we could consider a big hit. However, as the saying goes, hard work pays, and this was applicable to Dwayne's acting career. His first movie to become a huge success was *Fast Five*, which he starred in along with popular actor Vin Diesel in 2011. This American heist action movie is the fifth sequel to the *Fast and Furious* franchise that was released in 2009. Directed by Justin Lin, *Fast Five* recorded 626.1 million US Dollars on Box Office, becoming the seventh highest-grossing movie of 2011. These two actors created quite a bond in this blockbuster movie. Dwayne showed his interest to act alongside Vin Diesel when he stated that he had known Vin for a long time, and they had always talked about doing something together. So, he found *Fast Five* as the perfect opportunity to create a formidable bond with Vin, and we can say their relationship is still as strong as ever.

Dwayne continued to move strong, and made a name for himself by starring in the 2013 sequel *Fast and Furious 6* and *Furious 7* in 2015. The *Fast and Furious* Franchise became quite popular and a total massive hit on Box Office, with both movies making over 1.5 billion US Dollars. In 2013, it was announced that he was going to produce and star in an HBO comedy series titled "Ballers." The series was about NFL players who lived in Miami. By December of 2013, Dwayne was named the top-grossing actor by Forbes as his movies that year made over 1.3 billion US Dollars.

Question to Ponder: How would you feel to be finally recognized for your work?

As stated above, Dwayne was well known for his work ethic. He gave his all once he was on set to ensure the movie came out really well. For instance, in the 2013 action-crime movie *Pain and Gain*, he added about 12 to 15 pounds of muscle for his role. Dwayne and his co-star, Mark Wahlberg, had to increase their meal intake per day just to increase their body build. This just shows how seriously he takes each of his roles. When interviewed by *Muscle and Fitness Magazine*, Dwayne said that his diet was made up of seven meals a day, four of which consisted of cod.

Pain and Gain centered around three friends, Danyel, Adrian, and Doyle, played by Mark Wahlberg, Dwayne Johnson, and Anthony Mackie, respectively. This trio kidnaps a wealthy businessman to collect money from him, but things don't go according to their plan due to their foolishness. This movie was stated to be based on the real-life story of Marc Schiller, a Buenos Aires-born businessman who was kidnapped and tortured by a gang named Sun Gym. Marc stated in an interview that the characters in the movie didn't really describe those who tortured him in real life since the producers failed to ask for his opinion before shooting the movie. He was the victim, so he knew his kidnappers more than anyone else as they had extorted several million dollars from him.

In that same year, Dwayne played the fictional character Roadblock in the action-adventure movie *G.I. Joe: Retaliation*, a sequel to the 2009 movie *G.I. Joe: Rise of the Cobra*. In this sequel, Zartan has declared the Joes traitors while the whole world is now under the control of Cobra Commander. Now the Joes must seek help from their original leader. Though the ratings of the movie weren't particularly high, it made over 300 million US Dollars on Box Office.

Dwayne, After His Career Breakthrough

After the success of *Furious 7*, he played the role of Ray, a family man, in the action thriller movie *San Andreas* released in 2015. After a serious earthquake has occurred, Ray, who is a rescue pilot, and his wife go in search of their daughter. They try to save her before another deadly disaster occurred. The movie was directed by Brad Peyton and made a sum of 474 million US Dollars. Taking his career forward, Dwayne played a voice role for the character Maui in the 2016 Disney adventure movie *Moana*. His character was a demigod who had stolen the heart of goddess Te Fitti. He worked alongside Moana, played by Auli'i Cravalho, to restore things back to normal on her island. The movie was another sensation at the box office. That same year, he co-starred with another well-recognized actor, Kevin Hart, in the action-comedy movie *Central Intelligence*. The movie centered around how Calvin Joyner's life, played by Kevin Hart, changes when he reunites with an old high school classmate, Bob Stone, played by Dwayne Johnson. Calvin experiences a rollercoaster of events when Bob drags him into an undercover operation. Prior to this movie, these two actors had met at an award event and clicked instantly. They both had desires to work together on a movie project and finally got the chance to do so in *Central Intelligence*. It was no surprise how well they were able to show perfect chemistry in the movie. Not long after, these two reunited in 2017 for the adventure-comedy movie *Jumanji: Welcome to the Jungle*. The movie was based on a 1981 children's fantasy picture book written by the American author and illustrator Chris Van Allsburg. Available on Netflix and other streaming platforms, this movie, which was another big hit for Kevin's and Dwayne's careers, made a total of 962.5 million US Dollars. Dwayne posted on his

Instagram page how he was blown away by the positive reactions the movie got from the public. In the caption below the video posted, he had stated, "Grateful and blown away by your reactions after watching #JUMANJI. I wanted to make a fun Christmas movie for generations of families to enjoy around the world. I also wanted to make a movie for all the lovers out there. When the sun goes down, the sexy smoldering eyebrow goes up when you see the movie. Yup, nine months from now, they'll all be delivered #JumanjiBabies. Enjoy the movie!"

Both actors were back on the same set for the third time in the sequel, *Jumanji: The Next Level*, which was released in 2019. The sequel was just as popular as the first one, achieving high ratings as it also made a total of 800.1 Million US Dollars. Besdies acting in the movie, these actors also took part in its production. In an interview with Screenrant, when both actors were asked their opinion on the movie production and storyline, Dwayne expressly shared his thoughts. He had shared how he and the production crew wanted to be more creative from the first *Jumanji*, so they decided to introduce new characters while also exploring other *Jumanji* universes.

Dwayne and Kevin's interview with Screenrant

Dwayne and Kevin are popularly known to be good friends while having a strong bond in the film industry. Time over time, Dwayne stated in interviews that Kevin was one of his best friends. This duo is known to bicker at one another on social media platforms, and it usually leaves the audience cracked up. A video compiled by Sportscenter on all their iconic moments together was so great that Dwayne had to repost it on his Instagram page. He called Kevin his brother for life in his caption and stated how they would always be rooting out for one another. They even created nicknames for one another, Kevin being Snack-sized Denzel while Dwayne is called D.J. Both actors have appeared on many shows, some quizzing them on how well they know each other.

Question to Ponder: Do you have someone you consider your best friend?

Dwayne's Mainstream Success

Dwayne has proved to be an action icon in the Hollywood movie industry. He has starred in a lot of blockbuster movies alongside a lot of well-renowned actors. In 2017, he starred in the action-comedy movie *Baywatch*. Though the movie didn't get quite a lot of positive feedback from the public, he tried to defend the movie from critics. He played the role of Mitch Buchannon, a lifeguard who leads his team to investigate a businesswoman involved in a drug racket. The cast of this movie comprises notable actors and actresses, starting from Zac Efron. This high school musical prodigy plays Matt Brody, a recruit who keeps butting heads with Mitch in the movie. In the movie, there were scenes where Dwayne kept calling Zac "High School Musical," and this just entertains the audience more. On "Entertainment Weekly," Zac Efron was asked to talk about his co-star, Dwayne Johnson, of which he said, "He just gets better as he goes, like a flower that never stops blooming."

Zac went further to state how he has always loved Dwayne and found *Baywatch* to be a fun summer movie to star in. Another actor that stars alongside Dwayne in *Baywatch* is the Indian actress Priyanka Chopra Jonas. She plays Victoria Leeds, the corrupt businesswoman in the movie. Dwayne also reunites with actress Alexandra Daddario in this movie, having co-starred with her in one of his previous movies, *San Andreas*. That same year, Dwayne returned to the same set as Vin Diesel for *Fast 8: The Fate of the Furious*, playing his usual role of Luke Hobbs. In this sequel, Dominic Toretto, played by Vin Diesel, gets involved with a woman, Cipher, who gets him intertwined in the world of terrorism. The crew must come together to save Dom in this sequel. *Fast 8* was quite a blockbuster and big hit in the movie industry. The movie made over 1 Billion US Dollars and broke the world record by becoming the highest-grossing film in the first weekend of its release. This, however, marked the last time Dwayne Johnson and Vin Diesel appeared on the same set for the Fast Franchise.

Question to Ponder: How would you feel if people criticized you or your work?

Dwayne starred in two popular movies in 2018. The first was the action/science-fiction movie *Rampage*, which was released in April of that year. In this movie, Dwayne plays the role of Davis Okoye, a primatologist who pairs up and works together with Doctor Kate Caldwell, played by Naomi Harris, to save an albino gorilla and prevent two mutated animals from destroying Chicago. On a visit to the set of *Rampage*, Dwayne revealed that he was an animal lover. He went further to say, "I have a lot of dogs and horses up in Virginia, and I raise fish, so the idea with the first part about it was what great relationship with an animal in my life that I could apply to it. And also, the idea amidst the calamity, amidst the science going wrong in the wrong hands, it still comes down to this core relationship, and that's one of the reasons that really attracted me to begin with to the movie and to the script."

When talking about his other reasons for considering the movie, Dwayne stated how he was a big fan of the Rampage game when he was a kid. He had played it often while growing up and even after it was released on the NES. For this movie, Dwayne reunited with the popular director, Brad Peyton, who had directed two of his previous movies, *Journey 2: The Mysterious*

Island and the 2015 earthquake movie, *San Andreas*. Prior to *Rampage*'s release, Dwayne told the viewers, "There are some Easter eggs here, too, that I think people are going to like." He hoped everyone enjoyed the movie.

Dwayne's second movie, *Skyscraper*, was released in the middle of 2018. In this action-thriller movie, he plays the role of Will Sawyer, a family man, and former FBI agent. He works hard to save his family from a newly built skyscraper, the tallest in the world. Though the movie was considered a flop in North America, it had quite a lot of appeal to its international audience. Dwayne took on the challenge of playing an amputee in this movie, and he expressed it well. In an interview on why he took the role, he expressed it to be the most physically demanding role he had ever played. He went further to explain his bond with the story by saying, "The number one anchor with audiences all around the world is the bond of family. Regardless of race or culture or class or religion, the ideology of family is one everyone relates to. There's something very visceral about a family being torn apart and the parents doing everything they can to protect their young. That's always been a special anchor for us in *Skyscraper*, and for us to explore this on the canvas of film makes it so relevant to people."

Taking things further to execute his role properly, Dwayne shared how he had to consult Jeff Glasbrenner, a Paralympian who had lost his legs when he was just eight years old. He found Jeff's book to be a great source of inspiration for the audience to relate to his role. This shows how serious and committed Dwayne Johnson is to the roles given to him.

Dwayne goes on to co-produce and star in a biography sports-comedy movie *Fighting with My Family* that was released in 2019. This drama was based on the documentary "Wrestlers: Fighting with My Family," which was released in 2012. "Fighting with My Family" centers on the life of a professional wrestler, Paige, and her brother Zac, who both follow the footsteps of their parent's profession. While Paige's dreams seem successful, her brother keeps experiencing failure, making his dream unattainable. Dwayne makes a cameo in this movie as his usual self, The Rock. Though the movie didn't exactly make a lot of money when compared with his other movies, it got quite a lot of positive feedback from the public.

That same year, he teamed up with Jason Statham once again for the fast spinoff *Fast and Furious: Hobbs and Shaw*. In this spinoff, Luke Hobbs must work with his long-time enemy, Deckard Shaw, a British mercenary. They both must put their differences aside to work together and stop a cyber-genetic villain and also save Shaw's sister. When talking about his chemistry with Jason, both on and off screen, Dwayne explained how he tried to build trust between them. He would say things outside the script and expect Jason to react however he chooses, just to add more comedy to the movie. He also shared how excited he was to bring his Samoan culture into the movie. This was because it was rare for movies to depict or even talk about this culture in recent times. In the interview, he stated, "It's a long answer that gives you an idea of just how meaningful being able to showcase the culture was, and just really how many unique layers there were to it. Finally, we're just very happy that it worked well in the movie, and audiences were digging it."

Other than Jason Statham, Idris Elba also joins them in this sequel, playing the role of a villain they must stop.

Dwayne's Recent Movies

In June 2021, the highly anticipated *Fast and Furious 9* was released. The cast of Fast 8, who haven't reunited since 2017, return to the same set for this exciting and thrilling spinoff. The team is back together to stop Cipher, the cyberterrorist, who escapes from prison with the help of Dominic's brother. Originally, Dwayne was supposed to return in this sequel playing his usual role of Luke Hobbs, but that wasn't the case for this ninth installment. He rejected the offer to star in this spinoff and any future installments. The reason was because of the feud and friction between him and his co-star, Vin Diesel, on the Fast set. In an interview with *Men's Health*, Vin Diesel, the franchise lead and producer, explained that he tried to take a tough-love route with Dwayne to express Luke Hobbs' character better. He went further to say, "We had to get there, and sometimes, at that time, I could give a lot of tough love. Not Felliniesque, but I would do anything I'd have to do in order to get performances in anything I'm producing."

Dwayne considered his methods extreme and couldn't put up with them. Previously in 2016, Johnson had posted something on his social media page about a co-star which read, "My female co-stars are always amazing, and I love 'em. My male co-stars, however, are a different story."

It was later confirmed to be Vin Diesel. Though currently, the actors appear to be at peace with one another, the chances of Dwayne's returning to the franchise are very slim. This has made the audience sad with as some still hope he might have a change of heart in the future and return to the franchise. *Fast Five* was his first movie to become a big hit and attain quite a huge success, so one can say it was a stepping stone for his career into what it is today.

Question to Ponder: How would you feel being told what to do too often?

Although Dwayne didn't appear in *Fast 9*, he was in another blockbuster movie that was released that same year in November. His movie, titled *Red Notice*, is an action-comedy that was directed and produced by Rawson Marshall Thurber. *Red Notice* would be the third collaboration between these two as they had previously worked together in *Skyscraper* and *Central Intelligence*. The movie centers on the hunt for Cleopatra's eggs as an FBI agent (Dwayne Johnson) teams up with an experienced art thief (Ryan Reynolds) in order to catch the world's most notorious criminal, played by Gal Galdot. Though the movie was supposed to be released by Universal Pictures, Netflix acquired it for distribution. Becoming the most expensive film in Netflix's history, the movie went on to break several records after its release. It was the most viewed movie on Netflix on its release date, entering the top 10 rankings on Netflix as well as becoming the most-streamed movie in the US during the weekend of its release. Though it has been criticized by some viewers for lacking originality, it was the second most-watched movie on Netflix within 28 days of its release. It was stated that each of the main cast was paid 20 million US Dollars each for starring in the movie. Dwayne starred in two other movies that year—*Jungle Cruise* and *Free Guy*.

Dwayne's Plans for His Career

Dwayne has decided to take his acting career to the next level by taking the role of a D.C. Superhero in his upcoming movie called *Black Adam*. He has reportedly finished shooting the drama, which is highly anticipated by viewers who want to see him in a new light. Dwayne has shared how tough shooting for this role was for him. He took to his Instagram page and posted how he felt having to change his diet plan for his new role. He expressly stated that acting in this movie was one of the hardest he had experienced in his acting career. *Black Adam* is expected to air in 2022 and has been highly anticipated by both D.C. fans as well as Dwyane Johnson's fans.

Dwayne Johnson's Awards and Achievements

Dwayne Johnson has enjoyed a robust career both in wrestling and acting. He has achieved a lot of milestones and has received a ton of awards. Therefore, he is widely regarded as one of the greatest professional wrestlers and is one of the world's highest-paid actors.

Here is a breakdown of all his awards and achievements: Let's begin with his Pro Wrestling Career.

His Pro Wrestling Career: Awards and Achievement

1996: He won the United States Wrestling Association's (USWA) World Tag Team Championship twice with Bart Sawyer as his partner.

1997: He won the Slammy awards for the category New Sensation.

1998: He won the Deadly Games WWF Championship Tournament.

He was awarded the Wrestling Observer Newsletter awards for Most Improved.

1999: He won the PWI Match of the Year award. This award is given by Pro Wrestling Illustrated every year to recognize the best wrestling match of each year.

He won this award because of his fight against Mankind in January of that year in an "I Quit" Match for the WWF Championship. At the end of that match, Mankind did not have to say "I quit" because he had been beaten till he was unconscious. Instead, an earlier recording of him saying the words was played over the P.A. system.

Dwayne also won the PWI Most Popular Wrestler of the Year and three awards from Wrestling Observer Newsletter —for Best Gimmick, Best on Interviews, and Most Charismatic.

2000: This year was a year of several awards and accomplishments for Dwayne Johnson. He won the PWI Most Popular Wrestler of the Year award for the second consecutive year and PWI's Wrestler of the Year award. He also ranked as number 2 of the top 500 singles wrestlers in PWI 500. This means he was ranked above 498 singles wrestlers.

In this same year, Wrestling Observer Newsletter gave him awards for Best Box Office Draw, Best on Interviews, and Most Charismatic.

He was also the winner of the Royal Rumble this year.

2001: He won the Wrestling Observer Newsletter award for Most Charismatic

2002: Dwayne Johnson went on to win the PWI Match of the year award again, this time for his match against Hollywood Hulk Hogan. And he won the Wrestling Observer Newsletter award for Most Charismatic for the fourth time in a row.

2011: He won the Wrestling Observer Newsletter award for Best Box Office Draw and Most Charismatic. He also won the Slammy awards for Game Changer of the Year (he held this award with John Cena).

2012: He again won Wrestling Observer Newsletter awards for Best Box Office Draw and Most Charismatic.

2013: He won the Slammy awards for Match of the Year for his match against John Cena for the WWE Championship at WrestleMania 29.

2014: Dwayne won a Slammy Award for the category "Tell Me You Didn't Just Say That" Insult of the Year. He won this award for insulting Lana and Rusev. He also won a Slammy Award for Best Actor.

During the span of his wrestling career, Dwayne Johnson has won

- The WWE Championship 8 times.

- The WCW Championship twice.

- The WWF Intercontinental Championship twice.

- WWF Tag Team Championship a total of five times.

Question to Ponder: Isn't it amazing how much Dwayne Johnson has achieved in the wrestling world? It is even more incredible to know that he is equally flourishing in the acting world. Are you excited to learn about the awards Dwayne Johnson has received for his movie roles?

His Acting Career: Awards and Achievements

2001: He won the Teen choice awards in the category Choice Movie: Villain for his role in the movie *The Mummy Returns.*

2012: He received the Action Star of the Year award from CinemaCon.

2013: He won the award for Favorite Male Buttkicker in the Kids Choice Awards for his role in *Journey 2: The Mysterious Island.* After accepting his trophy, he released a massive quantity of the Kids Choice Award popular green slime on Nick Cannon, Josh Duhamel, and the audience in the first few rows.

2016: He won the People's Choice Awards for Favorite Premium Cable TV Actor. He also won the Shorty Awards for Best Actor.

2017: Dwayne Johnson was inducted into the Hollywood Walk of Fame in the category of Motion Pictures Star.

He won a Teen Choice Award for Choice Fantasy Movie Actor for his role in *Moana* as Maui.

Moana also won him a BTVA People's Choice Voice Acting Award for the Best Vocal Ensemble in a Feature Film.

He won a People's Choice Awards for Favorite Premium Series Actor.

Because of his role as Bob Stone (also known as Robbie Weirdicht) in *Central Intelligence,* He and Kevin Hart won the Kids' Choice Awards for BFFs.

NAACP Image Awards awarded him with the Entertainer of the Year award.

2018: His sensational role in *Jumanji: Welcome to the Jungle* won him two awards; a Kids' Choice Award for Favorite Movie Actor and a Teen Choice Award for Choice Comedy Movie Actor.

He also received a Golden Raspberry Award on behalf of the cast of *Baywatch* for the category The Razzie Nominee So Rotten You Loved It. While accepting the award online, he said, "We made *Baywatch* with the best of intentions, it didn't work out like that, but I humbly and graciously accept my Razzie. And I thank you, critics, and I thank you, fans."

2019: MTV Movie & TV Awards presented him with an MTV Generation Award. While receiving this award, he advised fans to be their authentic selves. He continued by saying, "We bring everybody with us, and you do that by being kind, by being compassionate, by being inclusive, and straight up just being good to people, because that matters."

2020: He won a Kids' Choice Award for Favorite Movie Actor for his roles as Hobbs in *Fast & Furious Presents: Hobbs & Shaw* and *Jumanji: The Next Level*.

While receiving this award, he poked a bit of fun at his *Jumanji: The Next Level* co-star, Kevin Hart, by telling the audience, "I want you to stay positive; I want you to stay happy; I want you to stay healthy; I want you to go to bed tonight feeling great. Because however old you are, around the world, just know that you are still bigger than Kevin Hart,"

2021: He won the 2021 Trailblazer Award from Hollywood Critics Association.

He also won a People's Choice Award in the category Favorite Male Movie Star for his role in the movie *Jungle Cruise*.

Dwayne Johnson has also received several more awards recognizing his awesomeness and athleticism.

His other notable awards are:

2015: He was awarded "Man of the Century" by *Muscle & Fitness*.

This same year, he broke the Guinness World Record for most selfies taken by taking 105 selfies within 3 minutes while his fans crowded around him on the red carpet of San Andreas's premier. Another person has since broken this record.

2016: He was awarded an ICON award from Mr. Olympia. Mr. Olympia is an international bodybuilding competition organized yearly by IFBB (International Federation of BodyBuilding & Fitness).

He was voted Sexiest Man Alive by *People Magazine*. He told *People Magazine* that when he first heard he was voted Sexiest Man Alive, he thought, "That's awesome. Wow, we've pretty much reached the pinnacle. I'm not quite too sure where we go from here. I've done it all; this is it."

Also, he was listed by *TIME* as one of the 100 Most Influential People in the World.

2019: He was honored by the United States 1st Armored Division. Super impressive, right?

The 1st Armored Division at Fort Bliss named their most advanced tank after him "Dwayne 'The Rock' Johnson." He expressed his gratitude by sending a salute of respect to the Blackhawk Squadron

In this same year, he was listed by TIME as one of the 100 Most Influential People in the World.

2021: He was named the People's Champion at the 2021 People's Choice Awards. After receiving his award, he gave it to a teenage girl identified as Shushana, a Make-a-Wish recipient.

Question to Ponder: Isn't it mind-blowing how much Dwayne Johnson has achieved in two demanding careers? Do you feel inspired by his story? What lessons did you learn from him?

Interesting Facts About Dwayne Johnson

1. **His Childhood Nickname:** His nickname as a kid was "Dewy.'"Dwayne Johnson, while recalling how he got the nickname, said, "When I was a little baby, I was with my godparents. I was probably, from what I'm told, six months old. And my mom had said to my godmother, 'Is his diaper wet?' She goes, 'No. He's just a little dewy,'" He recalled that for years, whenever he had friends or girlfriends around, his parents would automatically address him as Dewy.

2. **His Classmates thought he was an undercover cop:** At age 16, Dwayne Johnson was already 6'4" tall, weighed 225 lbs. and had a mustache. All the students in every high school he had enrolled in would take one look at him and assume he was an undercover cop because of his fast growth. Even the school staff thought he was too.

3. **He eats seven times a day:** To maintain his physique, he eats seven meals per day. He eats twice the calories that an average man consumes in a day. His meals consist of healthy food like broccoli, fish, rice, eggs, potatoes, and several other vegetables. He enjoys eating codfish a lot. In fact, he eats roughly 821 pounds of it each year. He also enjoys cheat meals like peanut butter brownies, pizza, pancakes, and other sweet pastries.

4. **He created the word "Smackdown":** Dwayne Johnson first coined the term "Smackdown" and introduced it to the world in 1997. In 2007, Mariam Webster added this word to their

dictionary. According to it, smackdown means "the act of knocking down or bringing down an opponent."

Question to Ponder: Would you like to create a word that could be added to the dictionary? How would you spell it, and what does it mean?

5. **He got arrested a lot as a Teenager:** As a teenager growing up in Hawaii, Dwayne Johnson got arrested a total of nine times. After his family was evicted from their tiny apartment, he couldn't bear to see his mother's tears, so he got in with the wrong crowd and committed crimes to make cash. He joined a theft ring that targeted high-end tourist spots.

6. **He is a Canadian citizen:** Although he was born in the United States, his dad was born in Canada. In 2009, Canada changed its citizenship laws, therefore, making Dwayne Johnson a citizen.

7. **He has a degree in Criminology:** As you know, Dwayne Johnson got arrested a lot as a teenager. Ironically, he holds a degree in criminology and physiology. He graduated from Miami University in 1995.

8. **He wanted to become a CIA agent:** At a time in his life, he hoped to fight crimes and work for the Central Intelligence Agency.

9. **He earned a Guinness World Record for his role in** *The Scorpion King:* He currently still retains the Guinness World Record for the highest paycheck earned by an actor for their first leading role. He was paid $5.5 million for this movie. Although it is not as much as what he makes per movie now, $5.5 million is still considered a hefty sum.

10. **He is a girls' dad:** He has three daughters: Simone, Jasmine, and Tiana. He enjoys hanging out with them, being involved in their lives, and doing things like tea parties and hairstyling sessions.

11. **He has a Minister's license:** You read right. Dwayne Johnson has a Minister's license from the state of California and is licensed to officiate weddings. In 2016, he officiated the wedding of his friends Nick Mundy and Dilara Karabas. It was a perfect and heartwarming ceremony. The groom was wearing American flag pants at his wedding because he had no idea he was getting married until he was already at the wedding venue.

The Rock officiating a Fan's wedding

http://allaboutbookseries.com/TheRockWeddingSurprise

12. **He wears different cologne for every character he plays:** Dwayne Johnson likes to play with scents and smells like what he thinks his character in that movie should smell like. He wore the perfume *Kenzo* for the movie *Central Intelligence* which he acted with Kevin Hart. And for *Furious Seven,* he used just baby oil, and "the makeup artists were instructed not to remove a drop of sweat."

Question to Ponder: Isn't it incredible how much effort Dwayne Johnson puts into developing his characters?

Dwayne Johnson's Timeline

1972: Dwayne Johnson was born on May 2 in California.

1991: While he was schooling at the University of Miami, he played for their football team, the Miami Hurricanes, and won a national championship with the team.

1995: He was selected as a player for the Calgary Stampeders in the Canadian football league. Unfortunately, two months into the season, he sustained an injury, and his time with them was cut short.

1996: On March 10, 1996, he made his debut appearance in the World Wrestling Federation. This same year, he won the United States Wrestling Association's (USWA) World Tag Team Championship twice, with Bart Sawyer as his partner.

1997: Dwayne Johnson married Dany Garcia on May 3 in a beautiful wedding that mixed both Samoan and Cuban cultures.

1998: On October 21, he made WWF history by becoming the youngest world champion after winning the WWF Championship. In this same year, he won Wrestling Observer Newsletter awards for Most Improved.

1999: He won the PWI Match of the year award, PWI Most Popular Wrestler of the Year award, Wrestling Observer Newsletter awards for Best Gimmick, Best onlinterviews, and Most Charismatic.

2000: He published his autobiography titled *"The Rock Says…"*. It was No. 1 on The New York Times bestseller list.

He made a Cameo in *Star Trek: Voyager,* in the episode "Tsunkatse." He played the role of a gladiatorial contender named The Champion. And he did his own stunts in the show.

In this same year, he emerged the winner of 2000s Royal Rumble and won 5 awards for his wrestling charisma and athleticism. PWI then ranked him as No. 2 of the top 500 singles wrestlers in the PWI 500.

2001: On August 14, his first child, Simone, was born. In the same year, He won the Teen choice awards for Choice Movie: Villain in the movie *The Mummy Returns.*

2002: Dwayne Johnson played his first leading acting role in the movie *The Scorpion King.*

2004: He was given the title of *Seiuli* by Malietoa Tanumafili II.

2006: He founded a charity that focuses on at-risk and terminally ill children. The charity is named *The Dwayne Johnson Rock Foundation.*

2008: Dwayne Johnson's divorce from Dany Garcia was made official. This same year, he inducted his father and grandfather into the WWE Hall of Fame.

2011: He hosted WrestleMania XXVII on February 15. This was his first live appearance on RAW in almost seven years. During this occasion, he started a feud with John Cena.

2013: He produced the TNT reality competition series "The Hero" and hosted it. Later this year, he played a major role in *Fast & Furious 6*, in which he plays the role of Luke Hobbs, a lead federal agent and a highly-skilled bounty hunter for the DSS.

2015: His daughter, Jasmine, was born on December 17. She is his first child with his long-term girlfriend (now wife), Lauren Hashian.

2016: Dwayne Johnson launched a YouTube channel with the name *The Rock.* The first YouTube video he released was *The YouTube Factory,* and it featured a lot of internet stars.

Later, he landed a partnership deal with Under Armour, an American fitness apparel company. Together, they created Project Rock, and the first item made from this partnership was a gym bag. It sold out in a few days. Several other items have been created from this partnership, including headphones, sneakers, and other fitness clothes. Did you know that his first signature shoe, the Project Rock 1, sold out in 30 minutes? His influence is breathtaking.

2018: On April 17, he welcomed his second daughter with Lauren Hashian, and they named their beautiful daughter Tiana.

2019: He got remarried on August 18 to his longtime girlfriend, Lauren Hashian. Also, he was listed by *TIME* as one of the 100 Most Influential People in the World.

2020: In August of this year, he teamed up with his ex-wife, Dany Garcia, and a sports management company to buy the XFL. They bought it for $15 million. They aim to open XFL training camps in January 2023.

On September 3, he announced that he and his family had tested positive for the Coronavirus. They had contracted it from family friends. They made a full recovery shortly after. While announcing it in an Instagram video, he said, "I wish it was only me who tested positive, but it wasn't; it was my entire family, so this one was a real kick in the gut."

2021: A television series about the life of Dwayne Johnson titled "Young Rock" premiered.

2022: Dwayne Johnson participates in Super Bowl LVI. He came in to hype up the crowd just before the Los Angeles Rams and the Cincinnati Bengals kicked off Super Bowl LVI. He expressed his gratitude for being at the Super Bowl in an Instagram post, saying, "Funny how life works sometimes. My football dreams failed, but many years later – they kinda came true. In a much bigger and more influential way."